The Essential Secrets of Internet Successes and Failures

How to Transform Yourself Towards a Goal

by

ESMONDE HOLOWATY

authorHOUSE®

AuthorHouse™
1663 Liberty Drive
Bloomington, IN 47403
www.authorhouse.com
Phone: 1 (800) 839-8640

Published by AuthorHouse 04/17/2019

ISBN: 978-1-4208-3249-5 (sc)
ISBN: 978-1-4634-8710-2 (e)

Print information available on the last page.

This book is printed on acid-free paper.

Table of Contents

Chapter One
The Desire to Succeed

The internet is such an outstanding invention. Who would've thought we would ever have at our finger tips so much knowledge and wisdom. I know you've probably heard that phrase many times over. It is true though, and economy can be dead yet residents can create a successful internet campaign and reach thousands upon thousands of people. Then once reaching thousands, even if they succeed at 5% they've still earned themselves a decent living. The decent living is basically a function of their goal and desires. More importantly their burning desire for success.

A burning desire for success, without it a goal is dead. You may want to earn a living in the computer era, however if you don't have a burning desire you'll fail one way or another. This burning desire is what will connect you with your goals. This burning desire is how you can succeed over the long-term despite any short-term failures you may encounter. Everyone will fail through some short-term seasons. Sounds gruff, however, that's where you will see you're burning desire pull you through towards you're glorious goals.

Let's take a look at desire now. When you think about desire what do you picture? Do you picture a child desiring candy, an adult his favorite dish, or the goal seeker his goal? Desire is defined as wishing, longing, requesting or petitioning. It's basically about having a passion for a goal. Desire is good so long as you're not violating anyone's rights. Be ethical with your desire. If you create a desire that's not ethical more often than most of the time you're brain will shut it out. The laws within us. That's why you need to create a desire that's honest, ethical, and moral. This way you'll be able to create a desire that will burn within you to create lasting success for your computer campaign.

Next create a desire that's simple. This way visualizing yourself achieving your goal will seem honestly achievable to your brain. Also, when you master desire you'll be able to create the same effect on the internet. This will demonstrate your ethics and morals to your clientele which will create a relationship. This relationship will bring you success from desire.

The media, especially this generation uses desire to the limit. People see a commercial that's specifically geared to attract their attention. The next thing that happens is that whether they need it or not they desire to have that item whatever it may be. This is especially apparent in children; they see a toy or a game, then for days they desire the product. The poor parent has to develop a strategy to calm the child down or to refocus his or her attention for the right. I guess it's a poor child too, as it's not like he's aware of all the effort into the commercial. I guess he or she could be fortunate if they convinced one or both of their parents. Goes to show the power of desire though. This is what we need to learn how to use to the full.

We're heading towards the basic idea of the power of desire. See, how goals are made as a result of desire. The customer see's the product, perceives it's supposively awesome traits, next it's a goal. It must be had. That's what we need you to have the mastery over so you can create a burning desire in yourself and your customer. Imagine having a product that was moral, ethical, and honest something you'd love to see your customers happy with and knew for sure it could benefit them in one way or another. However, know matter how hard you tried you just couldn't convey this desire. You yourself had it however you couldn't communicate it effectively.

That's what we need to work on next communicating with our desire. Creating a desire that's desiring to the customer. Your customer needs to know why they need what you have to offer. That's why you need to show them how this product will benefit them and make life simpler. They need to see your ethics though or they'll perceive you as just another sham or smuck. This is a workshop on desire so I hope not to bore or irritate you with the word desire as we learn more about its importance. So simply stop thinking about the word desire. Just joking, we'll talk more about state management in chapter nine. Remember how we talked about a burning desire to overcome short-term adversities, well hearing the word desire allot is one of them. If you presently create a goal in your mind where you'd like to be financially, or a place you'd like to be it should facilitate in overcoming the obstacle.

As we've all heard before if you want to be good at something you've got to do it over, and over, and over, and over again. Repetition, is the sure way to learn no matter what it is. You'll of course have to change your strategy for learning now and then however you're on the right track with repetition. You also still have to create a fun way to learn or you won't succeed through to reaching your goal. Many people create a desire however it's just a spark and not a flame. We need to create a roaring fire for desire if we are to succeed, then when we succeed our customers will succeed. The lasting relationship, that can make a person very successful.

Having fun with desire. When something is fun, you enjoy doing it. Fun creates desire. Isn't that what everyone wants, to have fun (assuming we're not violating anyone's rights). If you see something that's fun you want it. Imagine seeing your dream mate on the yacht of your dreams, with your favorite motivational song playing. Wouldn't that move you to want that yacht? To be the one for that person we want to create fun for our webpages. Doing this in a tasteful way though, of course. You must know your audience. Only, then can you determine what will be fun for them. So select a group you'd particularly like to attract soccer fans, travelers, you decide. Or check out a magazine and see what the successful internet pros are choosing to target for an audience.

This is getting exciting; we've now got a good idea, or are getting one of desire. Our customer is possibly starting to feel a spark of desire or even a flame, when we're specifically targeting their needs or desires. How do we maintain that flame? The answer is very simple even though the process isn't. The answer is by our ethics, morals, and honesty. Ethics, morals, and honesty you may ask. Yes, everything around is getting more and more crooked. However, we want our customers to see the difference, to see how we stand out from the rest. I mean the crook may succeed once or twice, however not for the long-term. Life always kicks in for justice. To succeed for the long-term we've got to have quality relationships.

Quality relationships are a result of caring for our customers no matter how young or old, naive or intelligent they may be. We need to be flawless so to speak. What good is it if you cut the corner only for you to be out years in the long run? You guessed it, it's no good. I'm sure your beginning to picture some good qualities of character which would make for a successful computer campaign. If not stop for say a half hour and just meditate on the type of person you could see doing well over the long-term. The person you will become if you so desire. Be courageous now as you can do it. I believe in you and so should you.

Feeling abit desirous for success now. Well you should as you've a good idea about what's required. You've noticed what a difference values will have over the long-term. I'm in no way implying you have no values. What I'm doing is assisting you in bringing them to the table for your internet campaign. See with your ethics and sowing bountifully as it says in the bible if you so bountifully, you will reap bountifully. Well, helping others to ethically create a desire will in turn create a desire for you, and the requests of your heart could just become a reality. Pretty awesome hey.

Internet succeeding or failing is in large a part due to desire. Normally, people hear of internet successes, or have an associate that's one. They then think well maybe I should give it a try it as so many are becoming successful, and even becoming millionaires as a result of the internet. Well using the word try alone is an indicator for failure. You've got to create that burning desire to burn all the negativity from regular thinking. This will leave you with your desired outcome of pure desire. The brain will only be negative or positive.

The decision is up to you. By reading so far I'm sure you have the main idea of how important desire is in creating a belief to move towards succeeding.

Going with pure desire. Now you have your pure thought of desire which can be transmitted to your customer. You are the capacitor. I don't know if you've ever seen the capacitor and fluorescent light bulb experiment. Well, the fluorescent bulb not even being plugged into a ballast will simply light up just by being around a charged capacitor. This is what we want our customer to do when viewing our site. We want them to light up with desire for our product. We don't want just a spark we want that burning desire for long-term success.

Don't you do that when surfing the internet. You see a product that looks modern, this creates a perception in your mind of how you might be viewed with your product. Maybe you see yourself becoming more popular with friends or family as a result of having this product. Or maybe you see yourself getting more respect or authority. Whatever it may be it got your attention. Society spends millions or even billions on advertising. This is why they are so successful. They for sure don't invest such gross amounts with the intent to fail. They (the successful) know how to have there advertising dollar go far. Before they spend millions upon millions on advertising they have a specific outcome in mind and are very good at reaching their goals. For example if you have 1000 leads every month from your site you know to expect that 1000 leads the next month. Next if you get say a profit of 5% from these 1000 leads you know that if you were to increase to 10,000 leads you would earn an even larger profit. Your sales would still most likely be at 5% of of 10,000 if you applied your same strategy properly and didn't apply any major modifications. So if your product cost $100.00 on 100 leads you'd earn $5000, on 10,000, $50,000. This could go on and on dependant on your desire, competence, and allocation capital.

Find your desire rate of efficiency, if you don't have a large success rate with a little most likely you won't with allot. You also have to become effective. It's like it says in the bible if your faithful in least you'll be faithful in most. Apply this to a rate of efficiency and leads. Your rate of efficiency will most likely stay the same as a ratio. So the more desire you create with less the better, plus the less you spend and the more you earn.

Feel like you've got desire down as we're almost at the end of the chapter. Your desire when mastered is so powerful. If you feel you need to create a better understanding read the chapter again and again until you can visualize a successful internet campaign. Write down on your internet campaign notepad (if you don't have one simply purchase a notepad for journal purposes) as many thoughts of desire you feel would be honest, ethical, and moral for your campaign, and the ones you feel will work for you in particular. Also, remember your audience.

Place yourself in your customer's shoes. How would you feel if you were in their position? Can you feel the burning desire, like a race car ready to do the quarter mile? Creating desire isn't as easy as many think. If that were the case everyone would open up a webpage and become a multi-multi-millionaire. So how do you feel? Write it down in your journal that you'll keep to gauge your success towards your successful computer campaign. Remember, keep a positive attitude until you see the success you desire. We'll talk more about attitude in chapter ten.

This doesn't mean be unrealistic, as being unrealistic is being immoral, unethical, and dishonest. This is just a second opinion though, however we don't want to halt our positive attitude. It will eventually undermine your self-confidence with the wrong values in mind. Being positive, honest, ethical, and moral takes hard work and allot of effort however it's worth it in the long run. However if you find your level of confidence, you'll be able to go from there.

That's another key point, finding your competence. When you find your competence, your framework is being set. Then once you have your framework you can add and delete how you like. Take your webpage for example, being realistic about your competence allows you to realize where your strengths and weaknesses are. Or if you feel you need a second opinion, find someone who'll tell the truth about you. If you have a webpage or not look around to see what creates desire for you. Is it tabs on the left or tabs on the right? What color schemes do you like? Do you prefer music or not? If you use music be sure to do things legal so your not copywriting anyone's work. As we all know copyright reserves the right to the owner and only the owner. This prevents their product from being stolen. If you remain ethical you'll definitely demonstrate it in your website. Which is as we discussed earlier essential in acquiring a clientele that returns for many years.

With HTML we can do many fancy things to our text. We don't want to over do it though. This would only scare our customers away. Like a resume keep it to the essentials. If your resume is too long you've ruined the desire, too short you didn't create enough. Find a format for your product that you feel will provide only the essentials. These are the essentials that will create a burning desire for your customer which will in turn create a burning desire for you. Enabling you to work towards your dreams.

Well we've definitely covered allot on the topic of desire. Don't expect to be an overnight success as no one else was. They may make it appear that way, however allot of hard work went into creating that burning desire. Look at desire as something you'll create for the long-term. This way as your confidence and competence grow it will increase your burning desire for success.

Chapter Two
Developing the Faith

Faith, realities though not yet beheld. It says in the bible if you have faith the size of a mustard seed you can move mountains. Well with our faith we will move customers toward our webpage, customers of ethics, morals, and honesty like us. Do you feel that desire is different than faith? After reading chapter one I'm sure you answered yes. Faith is another very essential ingredient for us to succeed. With faith we are able to have life pull us to our dreams or our nightmares, to successes or failures, we make the choice.

Well how do we create faith? First by creating a desire to have faith. Most people simply hear how faith is such an important ingredient for success. However, when it comes to creating a desire for faith, nothing happens. They then say well I had faith and nothing happened so I now know having faith won't do anything, how sad. Others on the other hand have set reasonable goals, and then achieved these goals. These people are the outstanding ones. This created a burning desire to wanting to master faith, as they saw it's enormous mysterious power. It really is amazing when you think about how you can control your thought process to succeed or fail based on your faith. Hearing that really motivates me and I'm sure it does you also. If it doesn't motivate you take a step back to think of a time where you've seen your faith pull you to an amazing new level of life. Well let's do this anyways.

So picture that time when you had a desire for a goal. You wanted this goal bad, maybe you were humble about it which is normally the safest way to go about it. The reason for being humble is there is never any reason to be absurd to go about reaching your goals. You can reach any goal by being a good problem solver, and safe. This doesn't mean you can't have absurd goals which are moral, honest, and ethical like you. Having absurd and realistic goals are both great for creativity of thought and motivation. Also, many absurd goals are only a reality to some as they dared to have absurd goals in the first place.

Anyways, picture yourself in a moment of positivety, if you can't think of one make one up. Take as long as you need to get this vision. Now go through the process of having the desire, creating the goal, and focus on what it took to move you to follow through to make it real. Savor this thought as this is the process of faith for success. Also, remember this for chapter nine as you'll learn about creating strategies there. Imagine harnessing that faith towards your internet campaign, having it pulls you towards unimaginable dreams. Or being able to create a desire in others, with your faith. You don't just have to use this faith strategy for your computer campaign you can use it for any moral, ethical, or honest goals you may have. We know though that if we want to succeed long-term we must, I repeat, must use our faith in a way that is moral, ethical, and honest. This way our brain will want to work for us.

After all it's human nature to be as good at something as possible.

Many people have used faith to their advantage. Which examples come to your mind when you think of successful people? Well whoever they may be, they used faith as an ingredient. Faith has an enormous pulling power. This pulling power will open the door to ones glorious goals. How bad do you want to reach your goals? After reading chapter one you now know how to create a burning desire for your goals. If not go over the chapter on desire again until you feel some momentum build within you (this is only if you feel up to it, otherwise please read on). This may all seem silly sometimes, however compare it to letting well meaning and ignorant people run your desires. This in turn usually creates immoral, unethical, and dishonest goals. Of course there are always some who could coach you also. Consider these as good role models who can accelerate your pace towards your goals.

So do you have your burning desire now? Good, keep that desire burning. So lets learn how to use this faith so that reaching our goals becomes effortless. Remember though, that to get to the point of where something becomes effortless allot of hard work must be expected. Let's not waste our energy as so much of life is out there, however it must be ignored if it's a distraction to reaching our goals. Distractions are bad goals. We'll go over goals in a later chapter. Goals in general are simple to set, it's reaching them that's the hard part. This all depends on the level of difficulty we decide to stretch ourselves to.

So do you still have your burning desire and goal? Great, or if not please read chapter one again. See, what I'm doing here is emphazing the importance of maintaining your essential ingredients. These are the essential ingredients for faith. Repetition is the hard work that is required for us to develop faith. Do you ever wonder why it takes you so long to reach a goal? Well, this was because your brain was developing the faith that you could succeed. Once you have the formula for reaching goals with faith you can plug it towards any goal. Our goal of course is a successful computer campaign.

So let's take our burning desire and goal(s). Write it or them down in your journal. One of the best ways to create faith in the brain is to write down your goal, with your desire. This is why you know you can obtain this goal. Can't come up with some reasons. Well make some up as you've got it in you to succeed. I know it and you know it if you've already done it well congratulations. Anyways you must decide to succeed with your desire. When you have the formula for faith written down use it by reading it over a couple of times each day. This will create a vision. A dream is a dreamers reward or vision. However you won't obtain what you can't picture in one feeling or another. Going over our vision will create a picture in the mind. When you have this picture feel it and harness it, as this is faith, realities not yet beheld.

It's really pretty amazing how we can create a reality and obtain it. Some realities are of course much harder to obtain than others. However, once we obtain the faith we need we'll use this as a building block towards our next level of faith. First lets consider a little more on harnessing the power of faith. Let's get that picture of our goal fresh in our mind. This is our reality not yet beheld. Meditate for about 8 - 15 minutes with your goal in mind. Be sure to get yourself into a positive frame of mind first. Great, now meditate in a way that builds your self-confidence for you to reach your goal. Remember to do this each day also until you reach your goal. Read your goal formula and meditate mostly before bed and when you get up. This will keep your brain ticking at night and focused during the day. Your brain has a large capacity, so use it as an advantage not a distraction to your present life. If we use our goal formula in an unsafe way it will be no good to us or our safety. So be safe by all means.

Remember, repetition and self-confidence along with our desire will propel us towards our goal. See yourself with your successful computer campaign. With thousands of customers viewing your webpage and liking what they see. Now set a percentage which will turn to profit from these thousands of customers. Be humble say maybe 2-5%. Once we obtain this we'll be able to reach higher levels or maybe the same just with increased traffic.

Chapter Three
Avoiding Scams

There are so many annoying shams these days. I guess I don't really need to inform you of that. Every time you turn on your computer there's pop up ads, or if you go to check your e-mails there's junk mail upon junk mail to be deleted. These all seem to fit into the category of spam. The internet users worst nightmare or one of them. Next, if you want to find an item or do some shopping you have to be so cautious as a result of all the scams. You can never be sure. That's the thing how do you really know when you can be sure? Some have used trial and error only to find out thousands upon thousands of dollars later that they were scammed.

When you approach a business on the internet check them out with the "Better Business Bureau"

(BBB). They are an organization that specializes in quality businesses, also if a business has had some complaints most of the time they'd know. My goal is to see you not get scammed once. It's a goal, however I don't know you and am not able to gaurantee you'll never get scammed. Use good common sense. Resist being hasty to purchase something from the internet. Normally a good business has been in business for at least five years. It takes more skill and financial analytical ability to project businesses in earlier stages. Either way there are no gaurantees with businesses, it takes a good financial analyst to determine the successes or failures of businesses. Hopefully the scams go out of business before you get to them. Use your common sense though along with your morals, honesty, and ethics. If you feel unsure simply don't do it, wait for a sure thing.

When buying from a company test the company out with a small amount. See if they're congruent. By congruent I mean see if you get your product that you paid for. Call to talk to a cusomer service representative or send an e-mail. If everything seems fine then the company should be legitimate. Always use caution. Keep this in mind when creating your internet page. Ensure you can back up your products and provide the necessary customer service for your company. If you maintain good morals, ethics, and honesty it will eventually be sensed and relied upon. A good reputation takes time though and can be lost in an instant. Be courageous though as you can do it with your faith.

Being flawless is very important. When your choosing a product off the internet, know what you want, then look to see who their competitors are. Usually they will have two or three competitors that will give them a good run. If possible call their competitors to see if they've ever heard of them. One simple phone call could save you allot of money if you were going to spend a little or a lot. This is all in part of being flawless at purchasing off of the internet.

Thinking like a successful investor with a burning desire to succeed. If you think like this you will succeed. A successful investor will look for companies with a long-term history of success. These companies normally earn a couple of times per share, with low-debt. These are companies the investor feels will do well over the long-term. After all customers will eventually look at your web page in a similar manner. You most likely won't have stocks right of the bat or even down the road (or maybe you will depending on your faith and desire). Customers will analyze your page like they would an annual report of a company. Also, I'm not saying you won't get stocks for your company if you do that's great, and I'm rooting for you the whole way. More importantly though is to have a successful company or internet campaign.

Thinking like a successful investor is very important. This is what will weed out all the scams for you. To put things in perspective if an investor was to place $10 000 in an investment vehicle and it earned 15% over twenty five years it would accumulate to over $300 000.00. The investor knows that if he was to pull his money out for say 5 years it would have a significant effect on the final capital. Take a moment to meditate on this point as it's very important.

It should assist you in seeing the value of making only correct decisions. We all fail, however if our goal is to be flawless it will really develop an appreciation for success, also a fear of failure. Some common things to watch for on the internet are the following. For one there are pyramid schemes for example chain e-mailing lists to generate large cash flow. Secondly, work at home schemes. These companies usually offer opportunities to assemble cheap products from your home. Thirdly, health and diet scams, pills that will help you lose weight with no effort or other products of the sort. Number four is the credit card repair scam which offers to cure irreversible credit problems overnight. The only cure for that is time and becoming financially mature, along with being fortunate. The fifth is investment opportunities which offer high rates of return with next to no risk, wouldn't that be nice. Lastly, vacation prize promotions, these are normally pop up ads which will appear saying you've just won a dream vacation or something similar (these normally require some sort of investment).

It seems people these days are losing natural effection. These people are definetly not being honest, ethical, and moral. When you think about some of the people which could get effected it's really touching. People like single mothers, families going through hardships, ones in retirement to the already starving student. Hopefully people will all use there common sense to keep away. It's hard for people living in these times, as wanting to better their present circumstance is normal. However thinking there is an easy way to earn a living will always remain a lie. If people want to earn a good living these days they've got to work hard in an intelligent and safe way. These people at the same time must realize there's no substitute for hard work. This is not to say we can't be efficient and diligent with our resources, as diligence is what will make one rich.

To become rich also you must be prepared to accept your vision. You must be prepared with the morals, honesty, and ethics necessary for material riches. Otherwise, you will fare badly, possibly worse off than when you had no money. Then the next time you set sail for riches your brain won't want to listen. The only way out from there might be serious coaching in most cases. Can you blame your brain though as you would've associated a negative experience to a positive outcome? We need to have our brain perceive our outcome as freedom from sin, freedom from our present circumstance.

Now let's talk about our webpage. We need our webpage to be moral, ethical, and honest. Doing this will enable ourselves to build a long-term list of clients or customers. We need to portray our ethics to our veiwers. By doing it this way we will be building a trust, not a noble trust, which we should avoid, but a sincere trust. We need our veiwers to veiw us as the one who wants to protect, educate, and see them succeed, which should be one of our natural motivators. The reason is we cannot reap where we haven't sown. Our customer has a desire to be treated respectfully, to not be scammed. He or she also has the faith, we must not pervert it if we are to truly succeed long-term. The laws of life will always catch up with one so keep the laws in your favour.

Next, let's take what we've learned from chapters one and two. Chapter one was developing the desire to succeed. Chapter two is developing the faith. Let's now develop a buring desire to not scam or get scammed, also to keep our customers protected when they're dealing with us . Have the desire to even educate our customers, to protect them in the future by letting them see what an honest site looks like. We are naturally like this, however we're just enforcing the behavior with as strong a signal as we can to our brain.

Now let's go to the next step creating our reality not yet beheld in repect to protecting ourselves and our customers from being scammed. Spend say 8-15 minutes and just meditate on the matter. Visualize yourself as the moral, honest, and ethical person that your are or are to become. This is another essential ingredient in our future successes or failures. Once we start playing with faith after a desire we are in turn creating our destiny(very powerful moves). Many think that they can't as they're victims of circumstance. That is a lie society wants us to beleive so the 20% of the population may receive 80% of the profits. The only victim we will ever be is the victim of our attitude. I hope I'm not sounding to harsh, however sometimes you've got to be to create the discipline necessary for success. To be harsh in order to realistically be kind is really being all kind.

We can be nice to ourselves and let us cut corners, however are we really being honest with ourselves. If we were to cross the street when we knew we shouldn't we'd be cutting the corner only to find ourselves inured or even dead if a vehicle was to all of a sudden appear. We need to be kind to ourselves in a way that will benefit us for the long-term. This most of the time takes facing the facts. This may be painful at times to do on our own. However, if we don't do it on our own society will definetly be more than happy to take a large fee to do this for us.

Calibrate your honesty, morals, and ethics like an engineer would with a gauge. See your min and max points to make sure these set properly. The best way to do this is to find simple situations you can work with. For example when you brush your teeth do you do a quality job? Take the time to be gentle and thorough cleaning your teeth. Use a revolving tooth brush as most dentists recommend today. Spend 3 seconds on each tooth going only one way, and floss (these are just examples, your dentist may tell you otherwise). So now we know what we're supposed to do. However when we brush each time do we do a job that's 100%. Ensure we're not cutting corners as these corners will only come back to bite us in the long run. They'll come back to bite us like a very, very angry dog so be careful. This importance of calibrating our ethics with something simple and essential builds confidence. Visualizing ourselves, or creating the reality not yet beheld builds a confidence in ourselves and others.

We need to be congruent long-term players. Being congruent, everyone knows or most of us do about the importance of being congruent. It is a very important part of honesty. When we say we're going to go exercise, we then must go exercise otherwise, we would be telling a lie. Is everyone congruent? Myself I sure don't think so. I feel this is an area society needs to work on, keeping balance in mind of course, as if you're too congruent you'll fry the brain of the person your talking to. So many times though can you talk to someone, they then tell you they beleive one thing, then the next time you see or hear them they beleive another. The reason is many get socialized into being significant in society. People want so badly to be excepted by their peers that they end up compromising their honesty, ethics, and morals. They forget that god will always be or needs to be their best friend. This type of attitude will keep us from swaying in congruency if we have faith. It will keep us from being swayed by anyone whether they be prominent or unprominent. Lead by example.

Again I realize were not talking about computers at this moment were talking about an attitude of success or failure. There are many computer genuises out there that can't succeed as they have too many conflicting beleives within themselves of whether to succeed or not. There are many quality businesses out there that are very inexpensive, find them and use them to your advantage with congruence.

These quality computer businesses are there for you to use. You should now be able to create the attitude and faith to find them. You already have the desire, as who desires to be scammed. It's only by our ignorance that we get scammed. We are good people, however we need to be outstanding if we are to stay afloat in these times. There is a large gap there between good and outstanding and I mean a large gap we need to get there though. The reason is that's the point where all of life is and can be attained with the correct slight shift. It takes being wiser than our present to arrive there as psychology is 80% of the game. I would mention some businesses for you to use however my goal is to assist you to think and act for yourself. Use your skills which you've learned to find quality businesses which are user friendly and relatively inexpensive over the long-term. This way you'll prevent yourself and others from being scammed. Also, you'll get to feel the true reward of using your faith and desire to not get scammed yourself and to protect others from getting scammed.

What a wonderful opportunity we have with computers. Computers in the era we're living in can literally make or break a person. We are to be the successes, and if we are to fail it's only at being a failure in itself. So be a computer success and avoid the scams.

Chapter Four
Creating a Successful Format

A successful format is another very essential ingredient to our computer campaigns success or failure. If you can imagine never being able to use your inner ability to succeed, how frustrating. You know you can succeed, however it just won't work for you. Having a successful format will assist us to overcome this obstacle. A successful format allows us to see our successes and failures or in other terminology our strengths and our weaknesses. For example if you were studying for a major exam which had say 15 different categories you'd need to know where your strengths and weaknesses were. Government exams are good for this at the college level. They will have many different topics each with a certain number of points awarded to each question answered correctly. If you were studying for all subjects and didn't know where your weaknesses were you could be wasting very valuable time which could determine if you passed or failed.

Finding your strengths and weaknesses is what will make an enourmous difference in your final grade on your computer campaign. See once you know your weaknesses and strengths you can next allocate more time to strengthening your weaknesses. This in turn with practise will make an enourmous difference in the success or failure of your computer campaign. We can do this by creating a success format, a format which we will never part form until we reach our desired goal of a successful computer campaign. Well, how do we create a successful format you may ask? This is by knowing your key ingredients. So far we've learned that we need desire and faith as the most important ingredients. These used in combination with morals, honesty, and ethics will take us far and keep us there for the long-term.

So let's start creating our format, get a workbook that you can use for this. Now on the first page number a list from 1-50, this will be our desires list, next do the same for faith, and lastly for our ethics. Now come up with 50 reasons for each. Take your time if you like, as it will give you better quality ingredients. These are the reasons for why your brain should want to reach it's desired outcome of a successful computer campaign.

Now on the next few pages over, as I'm sure you used a few pages there write a mission statement. This is a statement of your goals, your desire, and your faith in yourself with all your ethics. With our mission statement we are going to reach our goal of a successful computer campaign. I will give an example of a mission statement, you may use it if you like simply fill in the blanks where necessary to fit your formula.

The Mission Statement;My computer campaigns mission statement is to acheive a successful computer campaign by _____. I will do this by assisting as many as possible with my computer campaign. My computer campaign will succeed as I have an unstoppable burning desire to succeed. My burning desire is unstoppable. I know my burning desire is unstoppable as I have outstanding morals, ethics, and I'm honest, I'm also congruent with who I profess to be. I love helping people and they love helping me. My imagination is an outstanding tool for success. With it I can already see myself with my successful computer campaign. It's awesome, god blessed me with the requests of my heart. He did this as I take exquisite delight in him. God keeps me succeeding as I maintain my morals, honesty, and ethics. I love being such a wonderful person. I know I will eventually influence even the most negative of people. This will assist them to see how they to can become a success. End of Statement

So this is an example mission statement for you to use. Each day go over this statement one, two, ten, or more times. Go over your mission statement before bed and when you get up. Do it in a way that stretches you ability. Do it with lots of enthusiasm and feeling. This will transmit the message to the brain better, and over time create feelings of immense awe for god and his creations as you see yourself getting blessed with your efforts.

Also after reading your mission statement spend time meditating for about 5-15 minutes. See yourself obtaining your mission statement. Keep building and building upon your faith until your mission statement becomes a reality. Keep at it as you'll see faith, once developed pull you into it's reality. Then once this reality is realized use it again on your never ending journey with the wonderful power of faith.

Your format is like a directions booklet for a computer. With it you'll know how to operate your computer. Well with your format you'll know how to acheive your computer campaign's success. So now think about how many people out there that sort of float from idea to idea. They never develop true skill as they never develop the skill of mastery. Mastery is developed by repetition, repetition is created by doing the same thing over and over. This doesn't mean making the same mistakes over and over. It means that when you make a mistake you learn from it, like it was the worst experience that ever happened in your life, you ensure it doesn't happen again.

If we veiw our format as the power that it is we will really be able to start or become unstoppable with our computer campaign. Our format will give us the direction we want. I mean we wrote it so for sure it's the direction we want. We must maintain our honesty, ethics, and morals, this will give our format the momentum it needs. We must remember that we control our destiny with our format. If we don't have a format life will squeeze us into it's format. Or look at it this way if you don't make life pay with your morals, honesty, and ethics it will make you pay. What a wonderful gift from god faith is. Let's use our faith to the fullest by sticking to our format which we'll talk about in our next chapter.

Many feel that a format is just too impractical for them or even a silly thought. However, when you think of your outcome as the main goal it really shouldn't matter. Welcome some feeling of discomfort while using your format for success. You will experience humiliating moments at times, with failures use these to pull you closer to your outcome instead of further away. Also recognize your weaknesses with your format this way you won't have to repeat the same mistake over and over.

Making mistakes as we just talked about will happen as you learn to use your format. This will be like your fighting sword for fighting off your preditors before they take over your castle. Your castle being a successful internet campaign. The moment you forget your sword your enemies will over take you. Or look at it another way life will make you pay a crule price. How bad do you want to reach your dreams or your vision? This isn't a scam as it depends upon you and your efforts. If you want anything bad enough you will eventually receive it. Using a format also helps as your pace begins to increase towards success as you can keep your balance better. It will be like a high performance car which can handle the pace. Without a format you will lose perfomance as you won't have the engine and framework to succeed. Your format let's you create a vehicle for true success.

Now as your pace quickens for success you can handle it with your format for success. You will be able to distinguish where you are weak and where you are strong. Then and only then will you be able to build and build infinetly until you reach your vehicles maximum ability which is where all the outstandingness is, where all your dreams are at. You can do it.

Let's take a vision with our format now. Imagine you have your masterpeice mission statement. Take a few minutes to medititate on seeing your reality not yet beheld. Next, see yourself meeting some of the most powerful and prominent people in the world. See these as people who want you to succeed. Now see them one at a time coming up and shaking your hand telling you what a wonderful job you did with your computer campaign. It wasn't easy but you made it. You are now a success. See these people as your imaginary coaches, these people were there for you, ensuring your success. Or were they, you may think? Then you think again this time you get the vision that you know that god wanted you to succeed, yes you. How privledged. How does that make you feel with your format? If I guessed your response, it would be "amazing!". It made you feel amazed didn't it?

As we discussed before our format is our performace vehicle. We can supercharge the motor with more desire and motivation. By the way use anything that allows you to get a good understanding of the importance of the format. Or we can create a vision so strong that it feels as if we're in our performance vehicle at top speed. Then when we were at top speed towards our dreams a vaccuum of life kicked in to pull our performance vehicle at an even faster warp rate towards it's desired outcome.

If we want to succeed with our most powerful tool, "the format" we must be sensitive, by sensitive I mean we must realize what works and what doesn't work. We may have lots of desire, however if we keep wasting it on what doesn't work we will be wasting precious time. Along with time we will be wasting our energy. Energy is an especially vital source of power.

True, success with our format is so important. That is why we must spend from time to time a few moments just meditating on our strengths and our weaknesses as we progress. You will see it as truly amazing when you work past obstacle after obstacle. Pulling yourself closer and closer to your dreams. Our format will always be there for us if we give it the opportunity. Here is another example of why a format is so important. Imagine you see your social group, so you go over and start talking. After talking and associating for awhile you will begin to develop different veiw points, different desires, and different faiths. These differences could and most likely would alter your focus. You then go from having a burning desire to succeed with your computer campaign to not having one at all.

It's allot of times very hard to find associates with matching goals, desires, and faiths. However even if we have the same desires, goals, and faith we will each prove what our own works are. Our format will protect us both ways. How you ask? Well after associating you can come back to the real you with your format. People have difference after difference. If you are to maintain rapport with associates or future associates you will at some time or another have to compromise. It might not even be what you know or feel is right. With our format we can be polite give the situation it's grace, maintain our rapport while keeping our focus with our format for success.

I'll go over this situation in a little more detail as it's a realistic part of life. People may deny they experience this type of situation however they are only fooling themselves and others. We'll use the power position example. Say you've been researching a topic for years. Say it's the topic of successes and failures. You've read book after book, gone to the best seminars in the world on the subject, you've even studied the world's finest mentors, and talked with the finest consultants. You know success and what outcomes will appear where with certain desires and beleives.

So next your just starting out in business so people won't instantly beleive you know the format for success with mastery. You see them limit their own abilities by far, but since they won't show you the respect you deserve, even though you gave them utmost respect you start to lose your desire to succeed with you computer campaign. Let's also say this person is an authority in your life in one way or another.

Even though this person is in charge of you (maybe as a partner on a project), you know you could do that job better than they can imagine. If you were to go at this without your format your ability would end up being suppressed. Success would be lost the only thing you would receive is the rewards for being a failure. The reward for failure is absolutely nothing.

You know this now as your educated in respect to using a format so you use your format. Next, your desire and faith build, and build safely. You start to succeed creating more authority in your physiology, while maintaining rapport and balance as you relax. The reason you're so relaxed is you know you have the mastery as you've been using your format for success. You also know your honest, ethical, and moral. You know your top of the line.

The finishing point to this is when your authorities boss arrives just in time to see you perform the most difficult of tasks better than your authority. He thinks with efficiency in mind and decides to make a position switch. You feel awkward but again go to your format. Your getting to like your format by now as you keep succeeding and succeeding due to your format.

We'll discuss more in our next chapter on why we need to stick to our format. It's allot on format, however, with our format we succeed by repetition, creating a stronger, faith, and desire for our computer campaign. With our format we also free ourselves to success through the many traps of failure.

Chapter Five
Sticking to You Format

In our previous chapter we discussed the importance of a format with some examples of its importance. In chapter five, you guessed it we're going to go into more of why sticking to our format is so important. We'll then begin to appreciate more and more why a format is so important. Going over a topic again and again can seem dry at times, however, it's by repetition that we really learn a skill. We must focus on our outcome, as this is really a blessing in disguise for after all our hard work. We know we want to succeed with our webpage, after all we have a roaring fire of burning desire to succeed along with the faith to back it. We are ready for success, however we must recognize it when it comes our way.

How do I recognize success when it comes my way you make ask? Yes, we will recognize success when it comes our way with our faith. Faith is realities though not yet beheld. With our format this becomes feasible. Using our format in a repetitive manner is harder than some may think. Many believe it's so simple, you just go over your format and you succeed. That isn't true as you need to put allot of feeling and emotion into reading your mission statement aloud. The reason is this transmits the message deeper and deeper into the brain. The brain then is able to visualize our desired outcome of a successful computer campaign.

So for the first time lets take our mission statement that we've created and go over it ten times. After going over our mission statement lets meditate on our outcome for 10-15 minutes. While we meditate only do this in a positive manner. By a positive manner develop muscle with your brain, thinking only positive thoughts about you obtaining a successful computer campaign. If you haven't already created your mission statement let's go back to chapter four. I wrote one out for you to simplify the process or to give an idea for growth of creativity.

So how did that feel? Different hey. Almost sort of healing, like something your brain needed to heal or refresh itself with. How many people do you know who could just think straight positive thoughts for 15 minutes. Not allot, that's for sure. We have so much negativity in the world today. We must avoid negativity at all costs. Avoid it like the plague. Also, if you didn't do the mission statement practice chapter number one. Take a break and come back when you feel you could handle creating one. It's a wonderful tool in handling the normal hussle and bustle of life which goes on and on.

Refreshing ourselves and ridding our brain of negative thinking is what assists us in developing faith. So we know it felt refreshing, but how would you describe the faith or vision? Like a dot, a big picture or whatever you saw, is you developing faith which is how you can obtain your successful computer campaign or any other dreams you may have. Now let's do mission statement task number two. Let's repeat our mission statement again 10 times. Repeating our statement 10 times gives the brain a good positive frequency if we maintain an all positive state of mind. Next lets take another 10-15 minutes to meditate on our desired outcome of a successful computer campaign.

So how did it feel this time? Do you feel like your building a step which you can securely use to step you up in your computer campaign. Well, this is what you're doing. Be ready to accept your success as you climb, as you've earned it. Have the "how good can it get" attitude when receiving successes. It takes allot of courage on your part to have come this far and I commend you. This is avery suppressive and oppressive world we live in. Sometimes to bring skill and ability to surface takes more time and effort in some than others. We all have been through different circumstances, some for the positive and some for the negative. Going over your mission statement and doing your meditation sessions with a pure positive state of mind will really provide a healing and faith development for your mind.

It would be nice to talk more about computers with our format, however I'm taking the time to discuss a more important topic which will see you to long-term success. We've all heard of the phrase "take one step back to take two forward" well this is what we're doing. We're recognizing how important it is to have repetition and a format in our lives which we use on a consecutive basis. This format is what will take us the two steps forward. Finding the right webpage designer, and the correct html language is all very feasible, and relatively inexpensive. It does take time and effort on your part. What we're building is a motor and with our honesty, ethics, and morals we'll find true performance long-term for our webpage campaign.

Let's take some time now to reflect on a time when we had to learn a new task. When we were learning this task we didn't succeed right away. However, with a format you eventually succeeded. Well I'm sure you didn't call it a format with which you succeeded but this is what it was. It was your format which you went back to. Think of a time when you were younger and did this naturally. Maybe you had someone coaching you to your format, however it was you who succeeded. Let's focus more on the psychological aspect at this time. You had a task to perform. Your brain new what to do. You eventually became consciously and unconsciously congruent. Your desire was burning, your faith was with a complete heart. You had the successful physiology necessary to reach your outcome and it was natural. You didn't describe it as a psychological format however for success it was. See you're a natural and you didn't even know it.

So do we still have our faith and burning desire? Let's start again with desire. Let's create a burning desire. The kind you learned to create in chapter one. Remember, we need to be moral, honest, and ethical if we want this to last long-term. Good job, you've got your desire going. Now lets focus our desire towards using our formatted mission statement, our positive meditation sessions, and our faith for long-term success. It's allot, however your brain has a large capacity to learn. What you may think it didn't learn, normally, it was processed and stored in your brains unconscious department. This is wonderful to know, as knowing this we can relax and have more faith in ourselves and our successful computer campaign. If we don't believe in ourselves we could create impediments to our learning. We will collapse these though as we keep going over our format and develop a fresh pathway for our successful computer campaign. In addition going over our mission statement and then meditating for 10-15 minutes provides the brain reasons for knowing why to reach it's goal along with that it can.

MAINTAINING SELF-CONFIDENCE

Self-confidence is another essential ingredient to being successful with our computer campaign. If you can imaging going over your mission statement with negative thinking. You would still be creating a pathway for success however you wouldn't be compelled to follow through with your mission statement of a successful computer campaign. So let's take a look at self-confidence. The definition of confidence is the feeling of assurance especially of self-assurance. The synonym is a noun that denotes a feeling of emotional security resulting from faith in oneself. Note the word faith in the synonym. This is what our goal is with our mission statement to create faith. We will do this by developing a strong self confidence.

Let's picture in our mind something that will take allot of courage to do. At the same time lets remember our morals, ethics, and honesty. Get a vivid picture in your mind of something you feel you need to do but don't have the courage to do. Okay, now meditate on this situation that you need to do. Meditate for about five minutes on it. Now once you have this vivid picture break it up into 10 pieces. Then make a stair case in you mind with these broken 10 pieces. With each of these 10 pieces were going to work on our self-confidence in circumstances where we need to be courageous. Okay, so let's get step one in our mind now. Now focus only on positive thoughts where you have success with this first step. Take the time to do this thoroughly as it's an essential part of long term success. If you feel like you can't at this time take a little break. Don't be discouraged, as this takes allot of psychological effort, which therefore consumes allot of energy.

Now that your ready with your energy keep a complete positive attitude, and like a successful gymnsyst full of confidence succeed with step number one. The're your steps so you must picture yourself having success and bringing step one to perfect completion. If you feel you need to pray to god for this then definitely do this, use your efforts and creativity. Then when you have success with step one give yourself some applause as you deserve it. Next take a little break if you feel, as we've got more work to do. Success tastes outstanding, and you got a little taste. It's also healthy so keep at it, ha. Let's continue this process through each of our other nine steps. After success with each step give yourself some psychological praise. This will create desire in the brain to succeed even when the going gets tough.

So now you know you can succeed with self-confidence. We use such a little part of our brains capacity. It's nice to know with a little effort, and some faith we can get more out of life with our brain. By getting more out of life I mean keeping an all positive attitude which is empowering. Keeping this attitude in critical times is where you'll develop even more ability. Also, with an all positive attitude life has so many more options. So trust yourself to an unstoppable positive attitude for your computer campaign. This will be seen in your customers as you deal with them over the long-term with you morals, ethics, and honesty.

Our goal is to press on to maturity with our knowledge. Knowledge is the result of experience. With our mission statement we will use this knowledge to assist us towards a successful computer campaign. I'm sure your really starting to see yourself with a successful computer campaign. Maybe you don't see it happening right away, however you see it a couple of years from now. By applying the recipe for success, your finished outcome will be a succeeding computer campaign. We live in a society that for the most promotes fatty foods, by lots of convenient fast food chains. These meals are nearing 100% fat. To obtain this multiply the number nine by the percentage of fat. Next, divide this number by the number of calories. For optimum health we should eat at a level around 25%. If your wanting to prevent cancer eat a little broccoli each day as broccoli is very effective in fighting or preventing cancer. These fatty foods should almost have the same labels as they put on cigarettes. The reason being is they'll cause cancer if you don't get allot of exercise, which you would definetly need to do allot of to fight the percentages of fat in most of these meals. My point here is you must stick to your mission statement like you would a diet for you life. The reason is that's basically what your doing.

If you need to be on a diet of health basically to just be alive over the long-term it's worth it to stick to a plan. This is the same as having the requests of your heart or dreams. To obtain them with your mission statement it will take allot of work. This work is somewhat equivalent to the hard work of not reaching your dreams. You're still using energy just not in the direction of your dreams.

LIVING OUR DREAMS

Like a financial planner this is what were going to be like to reach our goals. We're going to save our pennies like an obedient child with outstanding, morals, ethics and honesty. Then with our planning ability looking long-term, ready for falls in the market, or job loss. Being ready by adjusting and being ready for items or occurrences that may have an effect on us while we keep our focus of a successful computer campaign.

If we plan 10, 25, or even 40 years down the road we'll get a good picture of where we can be with our computer campaign. Looking long-term gives a good idea with our format, as like an investor if he was to make some irrational decisions he could be adding decades to his timeline of reaching his dreams. So let's really take to heart the importance of sticking to our format with our goal of a successful computer campaign. Speaking of goals that's what we're going to discuss next. We're going to explore the fascinating world of goals. Why some reach them, and why some don't.

Chapter Six
Setting Goals

If you were wondering about goals along the way, well here we are. Yes of course you've got to have goals. If we don't have goals for our computer campaign we'll have a computer campaign that goes nowhere. Goals set targets for our minds. This in itself can be a success or a failure. To be a success with goals you've got to be sensitive to which way your brain is heading. For example think of a time when you were learning something and you were told several times what to and what not to do. Despite being told what not to do your brain still went in the wrong direction towards failure. The reason it went towards failure was that it wasn't taught the difference between success or failure on that particular task.

When we're setting goals we've got to ensure that we thoroughly distinguish what's success for our brain and what's failure. When we set a goal we must set it in a way that's black and white for our brain. Black being the direction of success and white the direction of failure, or whichever colors you may choose to use. So let's go to our journal now and number from 1-10. These are going to be our goals for our successful campaign. We will consider each number as one year. Then on the following pages write about half a page describing your goal of successful computer campaign for that year. This process will create a vision for use. Now for balance lets create a negative focus of what could happen if we were to fail. Maybe just write a few sentences for this if you feel. We simply want to demark successful goals from the failing ones, good job.

If you feel you can't think of any goals for your computer campaign, spend about 15 minutes visualizing in your mind a successful computer campaign. This will create some desire for thought. This is another area of importance so we must follow the procedures, as they're important for the focus of our mind. Also, remember to be moral, ethical, and honest with your goals. This will maintain mental health in our minds. Remember no matter what long-term you can and will succeed if you keep focused towards your goals.

With faith the size of a mustard seed we can move mountains. Also, faith is realities not yet beheld. So with our goals we want to ensure we're not wasting our time and energy or others. We need to be efficient with our resources (energy, time, and money). When we select our goals we want to select goals that we're going to stick to for the rest of our lives. Goals such as to achieve more are too vague. To achieve, I mean we could achieve more success yes; we could also achieve more failure if we're not careful though. When we make our goals we must be very specific. For example setting a goal to achieve 1000 viewers per month on your webpage is a good goal. To make it an outstanding goal add dates and verification points which you can use to gauge your successes or failures.

I'm excited to discuss the subject of goals with you. The reason is goals are such a focal point in our lives. Goals are the difference between leaders and followers, between successes and failures. We know of course that we want our computer campaign to be a success. We've learned to distinguish failures from successes. We've also learned the importance of desire, faith, and having and sticking to a format. All of these ingredients are like a motor on a yacht. Except the yacht has no specific direction. It's got lots of power though. Our goals are going to be what we move towards on our high powered yacht. With our goals we will determine if we have too much power or not enough, by power we're talking about our motors parts, desire, faith, and format. This would also include morals, ethics, and honesty. So does your yacht have the framework necessary to endure the tough times. Or are we going to be cautious and avoid what could stumble us? We'll actually have to consider that the average yacht can't go riding over rocks and expect to float. Anything that could cause us to lose our focus will be like a rock in the water. This rock could be people, possessions, anything toxic to our success. Remember, we're keeping our morals, ethics, and honesty at the same time which should protect us from allot already.

WHY HAVE GOALS

We've learned a little about why to have goals. But, why should we have goals? Shouldn't we just be able to go with the flow of life and end up a success? Do we beleive life will put us on top of a successful computer campaign? Or do we beleive life will put us at the bottom of a successful computer campaign? I mean why should we have to put forward so much effort for what others have seemingly acquired with ease?

Well for one, others haven't acquired great successes at ease. They've put much hard work into getting to their goal. They may have been around some successful people, where after being around them they learned how to become a success themselves. What if you come from a background that is more like a peer group to fail. Although the environment may not have been anywhere near healthy it still comes down to you. Many are in situations where there is a peer group with many desires for individual success, however that individual doesn't want to succeed him or herself. He or she must change their attitude. Although it may be hard at first it can be done. Once momentum is developed you'll be well on your way. For tough times use your mission statement, along with positive meditation sessions to assist yourself and others. Help others and eventually they will help you, or life will in an equivalent way.

Allowing our environment to shape ourselves is necessary to an extent, however you need to be the captain at sea. Life is full of surprises, if we're always letting others run our lives for us we're weakening our ability to succeed. Unless the persons a quality coach. Even with a quality coach he or she will want to stretch our abilities to set aspiring goals that are obtainable. So know we know why to have goals. We know that if we don't have goals, life will have goals for us. Life keeps going, it must be made to pay the price with your goals or it will make you pay the price. One decision towards a wrong goal can cost you years of your life. When your making goals ensure you are in the correct state of mind of a pure positive attitude. If you are not, then wait to make a goal at a later date, or change your attitude. We know we are in charge of what goes on in our minds, therefore we want to feel congruent reasons for making correct goals. A congruent reason being one to benefit society with our morals, ethics, and honesty.

ARE WE MOVED TO CREATE MEANINGFUL GOALS

Well are we? Are we moved to create meaningful goals? I want nothing more than to see you succeed many times more than myself and many other successes that are already much more successful than myself. However for this to happen you must never give in once you've created meaningful goals towards a successful computer campaign. Or for whatever you may have set goals for. Setting meaningful goals is like a rich blessing from god to show you his almighty power. God wants you to receive the requests of your heart. However, before he can do this you must let him know what your meaningful goals are. Then you must receive his favor by serving him with a complete heart, along with taking exquisite delight in him. He loves you so rest assured he will provide for you if you follow his format.

Once we feel our creator loves us and that he wants us to enjoy all that life has to offer for eternity that should start to create a thought process for some meaningful goals. Once we have this thought process to be successful by being moral, ethical, and honest we will start to receive many blessings from god. Then once we receive this goal thought process we should be moved to share them with others. Whether it be of our intimate group, or our computer campaign customers. As soon as we let life or one of its creations deter us from being moral, ethical, and honest we are saying that we don't want to succeed. We then won't as we'll have turned our most powerful asset and privilege against us.

GOALIOLOGY

Yes, I know it's a funny sounding word. With goaliology we're going to do something fun, we're going to determine our goals. What I did here was worked with physiology. Where physiology is modeling a person to determine what their doing, well with goaliology were going to determine what that persons goals are. So, now pick someone successful with good morals, ethics, and honesty. Now first start with physiology. Determine the positive attitude of the person, the feelings of vibrant health, and empowerment. Next feel like you are that person, with an overflow of faith and desire for a successful computer campaign. Feel the assured expectation of your reality not yet beheld. Now as you're feeling like you are this positive mentor, what are your goals? What must you focus on to succeed? Do you feel as you create these goals that you have enough faith and desire? With your mission statement, is this goal feasible for you? If not can you make it feasible? If you feel you can't but want to, work on you self-confidence first. Lots of people have made goals only to realize that they can reach them after they built up their self-confidence.

With your mission statement can you see yourself clearly with your successful computer campaign. You must be able to if you're going to be successful with your goal setting. The reason is you'll know with certainty that you're selecting the correct goals of your mentor. Maybe your mentor has an outcome you'd like, however has less the morals, ethics, and honesty. Well for this situation first commend yourself for being analytical. Next to create a positive mindset for us lets envision this person as a better person, a better person with morals, ethics, and honesty. This is a great step for overcoming fear, as who isn't afraid of becoming an accomplice to evil. This will allow you to be the quality, realistic person that obtains a successful computer campaign, free from evil and in possession of a successful future.

So how did you find this goaliology session. Did it feel feasible for you? Let's do this exercise one more time as setting goals is very important. If we don't set goals life will set goals of failure for us. We can always improve the quality of our life with goals. Select another successful mentor this time. Except this time were going to select a person that's successful at being a failure. So let's use physiology first to determine how this person is feeling. The person is probably feeling down or overweight. The person also is probably very angry and critical, with a very unrealistic view of life for the worse. The person just doesn't want to feel good about him or herself no matter what shape their in. Or if it's in their realistic power to change they don't want to.

When it comes to setting goals this person is waiting on life to make him or her a success. Except life isn't doing this for them. He or she still doesn't want to realize that they've got to at least set simple goals. Making no goals is comfortable as they never fail at what they put their mind to, and they're also made fun of less. They feel safe doing nothing, by being overly cautious they seem to never go about any goals. You are a success though so believe in yourself and ability to set goals. Being a success in reality takes just as much time and effort as being a failure. The only difference is that failures are in denial, they're afraid to admit that setting just simple little goals to start will really make a difference in their life. It depends on their realizing that they need to make a goal of being grateful for setting goals for success, as they're their own friend (ie; they need to give themselves a pat on the back).

After noticing the difference here we can really see how important goals are in our life. Life wants us to be happy with our successful computer campaign. We must allow it with our goals and positive attitude. We will fail at times with our goals. However imagine the person who doesn't set goals and still fails. The same emotion of failure was felt except one was towards being a success, the other was towards being a failure. You are a success if you believe in yourself and keep believing with you goals. In our next chapter we'll discuss how we can maintain success or failure with our goals for the long-term. We'll see the importance of sticking to successful goals for the long-term.

Chapter Seven
Sticking to Your Goals

As we just learned goals will take us where we want. However we are only capable of receiving our goal if we stick to our mission statement which includes our goal of a successful computer campaign. We realize we need this successful computer campaign as it will give us the freedom in life we deserve with our morals, ethics, and honesty. We're not girlie guys or women, or "woosies, we can and must stick to our goals. Must, meaning we take away any sort of retreat which could keep us from sticking to our goals. Your goal of an outstanding computer campaign is definitely worth the effort. Not to mention how success will change you into a better more ethical, moral, and honest person.

Don't people just select a goal and reach it you may ask? It seems this way at times, however, the successful person is only showing shiva. He doesn't want you to know about all the in between and slow times before success arrived. Or all the time spent dreaming, hoping, and praying for a successful computer campaign or what it could bring. He just wants you to feel like you can't achieve what he did. Well if he did then so can you and will you if you stick to your successful computer campaigns mission statement and goals of a successful future.

How can I stick to my goals if I must? You may ask this if you feel uncertain if you will actually reach your goals. However, notice when you set something simple as your goal you know you can obtain this goal as it is simple for you. You must select goals that are simple for you so you will want to stick to them as you know you can. This doesn't mean you shouldn't have hard to reach goals. These hard to reach goals will be there, however have them many steps away. This way you will build up steam as you reach each goal towards your successful computer campaign, or whatever else may be your goal.

Sticking to your goals is hard work. This is large in part due to the many toxic people or family in our surroundings. These well meaning and very ignorant people put you at risk of never reaching your goals. They do this by informing you to not have your goals, or they'll make silly remarks to shame you away from your pursuits and into their so called culture. These are so toxic as they create a negative attitude which is poisonous to your self-confidence.

Self-confidence is definitely a key ingredient to reaching and sticking to your goals long-term, however self-confidence can be a snare. Many are overcome in self-confidence as they never reach a point of certainty as to where the edges are. Sticking to our goals is definitely what will ensure we reach our goals. Sounds simple however, we must never forget that even after we reach our goals we must still keep our faith so that we keep our goals long after we achieve them. If it were so simple to reach a goal everyone would have everything they want. Many things like financial freedom, optimal health, and great relationships are all possible; however we must be sure that we're really ready for our goals. Maybe god is protecting us from reaching our goals as we're still missing a couple of ingredients that will keep us safe after we reach our goals.

We must find these possible missing ingredients that will assist us in reaching our goals faster. We must ask ourselves what will we need in order to be safe over the long-term once we reach our goals. Is it lack of morals, honesty, and ethics once we reach our goals? Is it that maybe we really don't want to reach our goals as we're waiting for our false friends to possibly start to like us? Or are we afraid that we won't fit in with certain ones we care about? If we are to reach our goals, we need a positive attitude that's 100% pure as we move towards our goal. The formats I am teaching you are formats which may be used for any goal.

We must also be prepared to not settle while we pursue our goals. So many start with goals particularly around "New Years". These people set their goals high, then settle for a feel good thought which quickly fades into a memory. The only memory we want is a painful past that will move us towards our positive future. To stick with our goals is definitely hard work, as hard as it is to earn money, health, and respect from man and god. However, with practice we will over time become naturals. This will be a result of repetition, the coach of skill and ability. The hardest part is sticking to our goals through the ups and downs of life.

Life has so many ups and downs. When we're pursuing our goals we must work hard to always work towards our goals, never forget to make good use of your mission statement. This is your map towards your treasures. When we experience emotional ups or downs we must ignore them before they take hold of us. If we do ignore them and stick to our mission statement even if the progress is slow we will get there. How lucky we are to be alive, a wonderful gift from god. Maybe god is giving us some balance in life so we'll appreciate our goals when we reach them or others when they reach their goals.

The hardest part of reaching our goals will most always be bringing things to completion. Bringing our goals to completion is where we experience a unity with our creator and man. This is where we must reach our goals through hard work and blessings as some things are impossible with man where there not with god. One thing we must remember also is that even if we have the whole world on the opposing side while we pursue our goals, we must have god, as he will protect us if we have the faith and give him the chance as he so desires to assist us. The bible talks about how he is waiting to show his power to those who serve him with a complete heart.

We must also believe that while we're pursuing our goals we will have many physical and spiritual issues, evil forces we'll call them, that will be out to trip us up. That is another reason why we must stick to our mission statement and our desire to reach and maintain our goals safely. While we have the faith that we'll reach our goals safely we must pay attention to how things are going. If we pay attention to how things are going we'll see where we will and won't need to make improvements, this should save us allot of time if we're diligent at it as we wont' be working on non-essentials. It will also make our day to day living much more interesting as we'll be more aware of what's going on in our surroundings.

Next let's talk about who to associate with while we pursue and stick to our goals. Associating may create or destroy our success. If we feel we can't trust those around us as we move towards our goals we must do without all distractions and those who could discourage us or infiltrate us with negative thoughts in respect to reaching our goals of a successful computer campaign. We either have a positive or a negative mind set. If we feel those around aren't a congruent or true associate then avoid them like the plague. Of course if you've chosen associates you don't want to lose or especially family who should never be forgotten learn to create the necessary thinking. This means develop a positive attitude that's unsusceptible to negative thinking. This will allow us to maintain the steam we need to reach our goals.

When we're sticking to our goals we're then making our goals an essential of our focus if not our whole focus. When we have this kind of thinking we will not leave our focus to the last minute not so important items. This in turn will develop certainty and momentum in our brain and body language. The reason for this is we're giving our brains conscious and unconscious mind the know how not the guess how. When we guess, we destroy the persistence necessary to reach our goal. With persistence, which is a definite essential in sticking to our goal we become even closer to seeing our goals come to completion.

So, why is it so hard to see our goals come to completion as we touched on earlier? Why can't we simply just set reaching our dreams as a goal and reach them all in say a year? The reason is we must be realistic when we reach our goals. This is hard to do as most simply set an enormous goal, that's more of a conversational item as oppose to a way of life and freedom. When we have goals towards a way of life and freedom that's where our destiny is shaped based on our decision and commitment level. However, we must stick to our goals for example if a person started out say $20,000 @ 20% for 65 years he would have over 19 billion dollars. If he didn't keep investing and holding his funds each year but rather spent the funds after 65 years he would've simply had another $20,000.

Sticking to our goals is like compounding money it may make such a difference if we simply give it the chance and don't give up. It's hard though as we start to compare ourselves with those who aren't saving and begin to feel we're doing pretty good. Then if we choose them as a peer group there could go our goals if we're not careful. It's sort of an oxymoron in that it's hard and simple to stick to our goals. Like the compounding dollars if we have an income that allows us to save $20,000 per annum and we know how to obtain and maintain a 20% stock average then we're on our way.

When we don't have one of the ingredients we must obtain what we need in order to achieve the return we set out for. This could simply be by studying stock market gurus and seeing which companies they plan on keeping for many years. Then once we know these companies we simply need to keep away from bad associates and evils while we pursue our goal.

If though we don't realize through all the hard work and discipline that we put into getting where we are then we'll let others, like friends, relatives, or religious acquaintances determine how we should keep our focus. This is where it gets hard as associates can have such a subtle and inadvertent effect on our future if we refuse to listen to what justice should be for ourselves. So long as we're willing to be moral, honest, and ethical listening to ourselves and god is the way to justice and freedom.

Then once we are in the habit of sticking to our goals if we give ourselves praise for doing good we'll create a habit that can't be broken. How fortunate we'll be once we create a habit that hypothetically with discipline and the right attitude can't be broken. This is when our conscious and unconscious brain will see the results of our hard work of simply sticking to well planned goals created by wise decisions.

This is also when we'll truly see that we really are on the way to our dreams. This is when we should take the time to feel the excitement that we should use to empower us to stick to our goals. Also we'll be honest when we say to ourselves that we really know how to reach our goals. Sticking to our goals is really one of the most important disciplines we can have in life. The reason being is that with the ability to stick to our goals we can achieve anything that we put our minds to. Without goals we simply wait like someone immobilized from the evils of life. It's not their fault however they've simply just given up on the desire to have and stick to goals.

Should we ever get to the point where we can't set or stick goals this is definitely the time to develop a better relationship with our creator, the reason being is that he will be happy to set us on a path always of spirituality and many other blessings. Mankind for the most is pretty good however, they can in noway set matters straight like our creator can.

So we're basically set in all ways. We can set goals for ourselves which god will assist us towards if we ask correctly or we can simply wait for god to direct us in a wonderful spiritual path that he has in store for us. We must always remember that our ability to stick to our goals is to reach our goal of course, so if we can convince our creator to lead us to our dreams then how much more wonderful life will be as we'll be sure to obtain completion of our goals.

Chapter Eight
Being Honest

As we talked about in many areas we must be honest, moral, and ethical if we are to be successful. To be moral and ethical we must be honest with ourselves. Many peoples brain including mine will at times develop what is called a scotoma where the brain will deny itself the truth to keep it honest. For example if I say that an animal I see isn't in front of me when it is, this is an example of the brain denying truth. Possibly I was in a position of authority in a park discussing to a subordinate that a type of animal is never seen around the park. Then to protect me my brain thought it would be safer to deny the truth.

This is were we need to be careful when going about our goals. We must never become overconfident in ourselves as there are always many effecting factors which determine our behaviors which determine why we behave the way we do. This is also why we must not be quick to judge others. Being honest requires a personality of compassion. A personality of compassion is what will allow us to be non-judgmental when dealing with others. This will allow us to develop a principled caring attitude (with effort) which will in turn lead us to see where we're not quite with ourselves and others.

Also, we must still be realistic to ourselves so that we maintain our focus towards our goals of a successful computer campaign. If we're not honest with ourselves and others we'll forfeit allot of effort which could've been used to pursue our goal more effectively. Also, we'll deprive others of reaching their goals also. To keep honest we must keep our mission statement, make honest and wise decisions while we realistically pay attention to the progress we're making.

To reach our goal we must realize that this is going to be no easy task. To reach a goal of success takes very great courage and effort. The rewards are phenomenal though. To honestly reach a goal is one of the most coveted positions as with it we may attain anything we put our minds to. Being honest requires that we take some time to know our weaknesses, this way we'll know what to turn into a strength. Not lying to ourselves may seem weak or impractical, or even very hard as we analyze ourselves, however, this is where all the passion for growth is. Don't forget to work on your self-confidence while you analyze yourself, not at the same time of course. Maybe try working on your self-confidence before or after you analyze yourself. This way, you'll be able to see what works best for you in a clearer fashion.

Also remember to choose your associates wisely. The reason is if they have a hard time being honest this could become a stumbling block for your development. We want to be around people that will stretch us for the better, however we also want people that are principled and loving. Ones with compassion as we talked about earlier. We might not meet their "so called" standards at the time however they'll still seem to keep us in mind. Also, if we can't seem to find people who we can be honest around then there is no one better than our creator who will always be there for us.

Many people have accumulated success through what we'll call a redeemed condition. They were given their way to the top. There's nothing wrong with being fortunate, however, if they didn't learn the required compassion then most likely they wont' be honest to themselves or others when lots of effort has been expended. They will take allot for granted and miss out on the feeling of figuring things out for themselves in a safe manner of course. This doesn't mean we don't need an instructor for certain areas. It means being honest and giving ourselves the recognition for a job well done. This is were we eliminate guessing which destroys motivation, which in turn immobilizes us to keep going ahead towards our goals.

Another type of honesty which is motivating, is to take a negative thought and turn it into a positive. For example if we believe we'll never succeed or that we're a failure we must replace this negative thinking with a positive thought backed by the appropriate amount of self-confidence. Maybe we do fail at what is our goal, however by creating a new thought pattern we develop a new honesty that is healthy for our mind. Negative thinking is poisonous, therefore, if we turn all our thinking positive we'll create a more wonderful outlook towards life.

Being honest in a positive way is also necessary for keeping ourselves safe. Have you ever noticed when your thinking angrily and not so honest that you seem to come much closer to danger. When we're more positive we're that much safer for ourselves and others as we know where the edges are so that we can be honest.

Many people view honesty as something to apply when they like and with whom they like. This is an unfortunate gross injustice which is very prevalent in society today. The ones who need the justice and should receive it are the ones denied it due to many fraudulent and greedy business people. When we decide to commit to being honest we'll be able to protect ourselves better as we learn to develop the compassion to help others. Many people today find themselves in many injurious situations only because they failed to be honest, moral, and ethical.

The people who have learned to become honest have developed true skill on how to succeed in this day and age amongst many crooked people with no natural affection. These ones, who developed the skill, like any, experienced set backs; however, with time and effort, learned to succeed the crooked by far and for a much longer time possibly their whole lifetime or a good part of it. Being honest is very hard, especially in relation to earning an honest living, the reason being is there is such an evil influence in the world today, everyone or most want immediate gratification. They see all the so called rich, then compare themselves and deny envy. This envy in turn generates a greed which seems to disillusion many at some point in time.

To prepare ourselves for being honest, we must become better planners. With a planning attitude we'll be planning our goals and not what we think will make us happy in the moment. With planning our goals we develop skill and ability within ourselves. We also protect ourselves from being the "Jones" experimental guinea pig as they would watch and learn if we were trying to keep up, only to be feeding more success for them.

When we plan with being honest, ethical, and moral we free ourselves from many of the day to day stresses. We do this by letting our brains conscious and unconscious mind know where we're heading. This is again why it's useful to use our mission statement. With a plan we don't get misdirected as much as we normally could in life. Our plan allows us to be a congruent person. It also allows us to gauge our success.

Gauging our success is very important. When we gauge our success we let our brain know how we are doing. We also let our brain know whether or not we need to improve with our state of mind and strategy. Going about goals is hard work, our brain will protect us (or so it thinks) from succeeding if we offset another important part of our life. For example say we have a six figure income, or a seven figure income, as a balanced goal. However, in our subconscious mind we feel that reaching these goals will offset our morals, ethics, and honesty, this is an example of incongruence of thought. I'm just touching lightly on some important points brought out more thoroughly in neuro-linguistic programming. NLP is basically a manual for how the brain works. It's really a very fascinating subject.

So as we're learning it's very important to keep honest while being moral, honest, and ethical. This will eliminate guessing which will create motivation for us. With strong motive we are able to overcome all obstacles if we're careful in the process. We will talk more about the importance of motivation in our next chapter.

Life being realistic can be very wonderful once figured out. However, if we're following many lies we might be wasting allot of life. Avoiding lies is very common sense, and very important. The computer world today as we discussed in chapter three is filled with scams. These scams are basically acts of cruelty to the many naive ones in the world today. Self-defense techniques of honesty are definitely needed to protect ourselves in these extremely critical times, just as the bible prophesied we are living in critical times.

Now, let's take some time to realize how wonderful we are as a humans no matter what shape, size or color we are. We're honest, moral and ethical, right? Yes, of course we all need to work on some areas however, we must find that wonderful core person inside of us. So let's get into a positive state of mind.

Remember a time when you were doing your favorite thing to do. At first it will probably seem weak to you as you most likely won't be able to hold your state of mind for long. However, we need to start somewhere. If it seems like you can't do it consciously then try a more unconscious approach where it's almost like you don't realize it in the NLP language this is called conscious incompetence. The other of course is called unconscious competence where it's more natural, whichever works though.

Now when you get your positive state really feel what your feeling. This is the state of mind where if the thoughts are moral, ethical, and honest you can really start moving towards the correct direction if your ready to take action with your motivation, and attitude which we'll discuss further in chapters nine and ten.

Realizing how wonderful of a person we are is being honest if we choose to be. We all fall short of the glory of god in our lives at some point each day however it's our attitude which is so important. It can steer us into or away from danger. There are so many different ways to look at life with our attitude. So if were in a positive state with ourselves and others we increase our chance of a successful computer campaign if it happens at all. Sounds doubtful yes, well controlling our states of mind will determine if we're successful or not long-term. If we're honest in a positive state of mind, repeating our strategy over until we succeed will take us there. We will of course have to make adjustments now and then. We'll need to be prepared though, to adjust for success as many times as it takes.

Let's take another look at what a wonderful person we are no matter what our personality is like. Also, think about what would cause you to become an even better person as you grow towards your successful computer campaign. Focus on you nominalizations for things. Nominalizations are things like wealth, success, fun, health, ecstasy, love, learning, exercising to mention a few. These determine how we behave and who we choose to do them with. Nominalizations can really effect our decisions. These are very powerful thoughts that we make honest decisions about. Nominalizations create barriers for us and others. We might feel that for us to be a somebody we have to earn x amount of money or have x amount of looks.

These categories are important however we must use them to our advantage with our personality. We must also do this in a way that doesn't violate anyones rights. People all have a right to be the type of person they choose to be, in gods eyes we're all free moral agents also. He's the one that really counts more than anyone. With our computer campaign we will need to consider and be honest about our customers and their nominalizations. This is basically what has to happen for them to be convinced. Now they hopefully already know that we're honest, ethical, and moral. If they don't and we want their business we will have to work hard at meeting their nominalizations if we want to succeed with them long-term (or long enough to reach our dreams or goals) which is of course our goal.

Being honest about ours and other peoples nominalizations will create meaningful and quality relationships. The kind we all long for as they meet all of our human needs. When our human needs, which are what has to happen in success, marriage (if at all), career, safety, etc are met we feel we can let our guard down as this is what we've been waiting for. However, people who abuse the power of pretending to be honest, ethical, and moral are a disgrace to the wonders of human behavior (to be interpreted as a therapeutic term). They cheat themselves and others of skills that need to be acquired and developed, they usually end up like a cat chasing its tail, going around and around, as they refuse to grow up, or so they think others need to, as they simply won't be honest. You my friend are above and beyond dishonesty, and ready to take your life to the next level if you honestly put your mind to it.

Chapter Nine
Getting the Motivation

Getting the motivation. Another title I might have used for this chapter would be "Getting the Vision", which is essentially what we're doing. When we're getting motivated we're creating a visionary course that we must follow to reach our goal. Motivation has many ingredients, using modalities which are; visual, auditory, kinesthetic, olfactory, and gustatory. Motivation also uses sub-modalities like near, far, hot, cold, dark bright to mention a few. We process these modalities and sub-modalities in ways that either empower or disempower us. They create our attitude which determines how we feel. We are in charge if we know how to create the appropriate frame of mind in an instant. Emotions are in charge if we don't. It's equivalent to a drunk driver basically, someone driving a physical body unaware for the critical and most important moments.

We must completely take charge of our emotions and make life pay instead of it making us be it's victim. We can with our modalities and sub-modalities. So first create a positive picture in your mind of a successful computer campaign. Visualize, hear, and feel how you'll feel when you reach this successful computer campaign. Hold this state for many minutes, possibly think of your favorite song as this will instantly allow your subconscious mind to get in on the action of thought. Next, feel the congruence of your conscious and unconscious minds. Feel it and hold it again for a few minutes. This will allow you to develop competence at holding your thoughts in a positive state of certainty if done right. I know with repetition this skill can easily be mastered. What most don't realize is that they do this naturally allot of times in a negative way where they then try to make themselves feel good by eating, smoking, drinking, or misbehaving, unethically, immorally or dishonestly.

With being able to control our frame of mind we develop a more positive outlook on life, feeling more inner joy. These feelings are awesome natural feelings and create a desire, which then creates a motive to move towards our goals where we reach them in a moral, honest, and ethical way. This in turn brings dignity and respect to ourselves, god, and others in our lives.

We also may know how or what to do regarding some basics of motivation, however without energy we're nothing. Without 20% body water we can last only a short while before we would die or experience serious problems. Even worse is oxygen depletion, without oxygen our cells lose power and stop functioning almost immediately. Our cells and blood are both very crucial to our energy levels. If we want and need motivation which we certainly do we must take very good care of our bodies. The best diet possible is vegetarian and don't worry about getting protein as when you eat broccoli you're getting 47% protein. Keep balanced though, and do your research or use a valuable source before making any decisions.

Now that we're thinking naturally about getting motivated in a moral, honest, and ethical, way let's get back to some exercises using modalities and sub-modalities. Modalities and sub-modalities are really very powerful to our advantage when we use them properly. The reason is we can basically place ourselves into any state of mind we desire using our god given qualities.

So lets move on to some exercises using modalities and sub-modalities. Ensure you have energy for this and are in a more aerobic state of mind, or playful anyways. Our goal here is to be able to create and hold any state of mind we desire using both our conscious and unconscious minds. One other item we will need is physiology. Physiology is how we move our body. How we move our body has a very, very significant impact on our mind and attitude.

Okay, so get out a pen and some paper. Next right down visual, auditory, and kinesthetic with ten spaces between each category. I know our goal is to have a successful computer campaign, however, we're working on states of mind here so I'm going to pick a topic for us to work on. Let's work on the topic of being loving and attracting love in our lives in one way or another. So under each category write down five moral, honest, and ethical ways to attract and create love in a visual, auditory, and kinesthetic mode. Now, when you've finished think and realize what you've written down as these are you're nominalizations of what has to happen for you to feel love and attract love in a visual, auditory, and kinesthetic mode. The reason is these are our real feelings in a natural state and basically we must feel these emotions in a way of success, career, relationship, or other nominalizational form for us to feel love. Therefore a congruence needs to be met between the emotion and nominalization.

Now let's make another list of 5 sub-modalities for each category. Remember sub-modalities are things like close, near, dark or bright, hot or cold. Sub-modalities basically create more or less feeling for our modalities. Sub-modalities use categories which can be described with nominalizations also. These are verbs that are changed into an abstract noun. These are also ways of describing a feeling of what specifically needs to happen for us to feel loved and to feel like giving love.

To create thought ask your brain questions that are requiring a specific answer. These are very useful in getting clarity for our categories. The more specific we are the more we'll feel certain that we're actually feeling loved or are being loved. Therefore someone else will feel more love also. Being more specific will build more motivation as guessing and uncertainty can quickly turn into a fear if we're not careful.

Okay, so we've basically figured out what needs to happen for us to feel loved and to give love. Let's take down the strategy though. So if when you want to show love to someone you say " I love you", you would note that down as (Ai), auditory internal. As an example I'll just show what a finished strategy might look like Ve>Ae>Ke. In this situation I pictured a man with his wife. Here the man looked at his wife lovingly, (Ve) with warmth, then he said "honey, I love you", (Ae), as he gave his wife a hug and kiss (Ke).

Great, so now we have the idea of creating a strategy. Lets now create a strategy for thinking creatively. This one I feel is just awesome for creating motivation that will keep someone moving toward a goal. We'll call it the motivator. For the motivator we have three different states of mind, the optimist, the judge, and the realist. We will need to have three states of mind. I want freedom for you and so do you so ensure to figure out how you get into these states.

So first get into an optimistic state of mind. Think as if you have no limits, as if absolutely nothing could stop you from reaching your successful computer campaign or whatever else you'd like to reach as a goal. Realize also that we will be going into 2 other states of mind the realist, and the judge. That's right, they will be coming in to attempt to prevent us from being optimistic. We're free from them now so get out your favourite song or hear it inside of you, or do both.

Remember, you're unstoppable, all of life is obtainable for you as you are in charge and reach every goal you set out for. You are it, everyone loves you, and you love you, god loves you, and you love life and everything about it. Your morals, ethics, and honesty are outstanding. People see you and wonder how you always seem to make it happen.

Let's keep thinking optimistically. Life wants to stop you sometimes however you know you always reach all you goals so you let it pass like a bad season. Then when it's gone it's like your spring loaded from the amount of energy you pushed down due to a bad season. Now feel yourself spring with more love, joy, happiness, ecstasy, all of your favorite emotions. Feel the emotions building and building themselves upon each other. Feel as if what your doing is just and righteous, feel like you see gods rays of light shining upon you with angels also looking at you.

These angels are mighty and powerful, you have the ability to reach any goal, however, if you ever needed a hand one of the super powerful angels would make anything happen for you as you're moral, honest, and ethical. Also, god your creator loves you, and you know he'd do anything for you. You're unstoppable. I love you, and god loves you!, say it ten times to yourself or out loud. Feel your brain just snapping into a positive state of mind as it floods itself with all the healing of the positive emotions.

Okay, now keep your state and realize what your feeling and how your feeling it. Write down if it's Ve, Vi, Ai, Ae, Ki, or Ke. Remember these are your modalities. What were doing here is capturing the formula for how we are when we're thinking optimistically. This way we'll simply be able to do exactly what our formula is and feel great anytime with ease.

Okay, now the judge in you is coming out. Feel like you are an authority and that thinking optimistically is only for frauds. Feel that if someone is thinking optimistically that they must be immoral, unethical, and dishonest, feel it. Notice the sudden change in physiology. Feel abit angry, so that you become critical. Notice that when your angry you quickly become a very critical person. This person is wise, very wise and feels he or she needs to learn nothing from nobody.

Keep thinking in the judge state of mind. Notice all of your positive creativity going. How do you feel? Do you feel like going towards any positive goals? Probably not, as you feel that optimistic thinking is for crooks. Feel it, feel how you think the world should be, and is, in a negative state of mind. Feel how people feel about you.

Now, in the judge state of mind feel love while you're angry. Feel the brokenness of heart. Yes, you'll still feel like god is with you, however isn't it a shame. People they just don't know how to do what's right, if they could only face the facts. Okay, hold your state of mind and write down your strategy. Use your visual, auditory, and kinesthetic modalities. Remember, this is another strategy that we need to create in order for us to feel the motivator inside.

Okay, remember the last sentence before we wrote down our last strategy. We said "people, they just don't know how to do what's right, if they could only face the facts". Here he or she becomes the realist. Now we are the realist. Everything has to be realistic. We appreciate being positive, however we need to be realistic. This is the awesome part. We can think optimistically, however we must have a realistic plan to reach our goals. So let's keep being realistic. When we're realistic how do we feel about performing a task? Do we feel that it's feasible. Well that depends, we most likely said, as it depends if it's realistic or not. If it's not realistic then it can't be done.

This is where we need to allow ourselves some slack to think. We need to realize that if anyone else in the whole world has performed this moral, ethical, and honest task then so can we. We just need to be realistic and to figure out their strategy. We could do this by asking them suitable questions that could lead us towards the same outcome in a realistic time frame. So as we're still realistic let's take down our strategy. Now we are set, we have our optimist, judge, and realist whenever we want. This is because we have the strategy for success for each state of mind.

So which state of mind did you like the best. Probably the optimist. These are all good states of mind for creativity. When we are creative we are motivated. When we are motivated we move towards our goals, we get where we want to get in life and with who we want.

Let's briefly talk about how to use each of these states as a balance towards reaching our goals. To be the motivator our goal is to get so motivated that we're actually moved. We need to create a balance between the optimist, the judge, and the realist. Imagine that we see a 100% figure. Now, break this down into three even parts which is 33.33% for each state of mind, this is just the start.

We need to find a balance that leverages us to move ahead towards our goals. This might be 60% optimist, 10% judge, and 30 % realist. Remember to use the realist as a planner for your success, great job. We discussed some pretty important topics in this chapter. These are more basic topics on development, however slight shifts make all the difference. That is what we're going to discuss next in chapter ten. We'll discuss how attitude and physiology make enormous differences in accomplishment by simple shifts in attitude. So let's go over to our final chapter for this book, chapter ten.

Chapter Ten
Developing the Attitude

Developing the attitude is another very important aspect of reaching our goal of a successful computer campaign, or any other goal we may have. Like a pilot with his airplane so we are with our attitude we're either pulling up towards our goal or down towards a miserable crash landing. That is why it's so important that we maintain a positive attitude.

Maintaining or developing a positive attitude is no easy task. We live in a society that is so train track driven. A group normally just hop on a negative thought track and except it as life. You, for coming this far are obviously not like that, you're a winner. I also congratulate you for coming this far. These people really only have one direction towards the easy way out. For example, look at all the people who on a regular basis filter through fast food restaurants. These people are almost digging their grave, or are poisoning themselves with many toxins. There body may take months to eliminate these toxins.

The reason so many people don't take charge of their lives is because their basically denying that they have any problems. This is similar to someone in a bad relationship where the person is simply just pulling themselves down emotionally. It's very hard to get out of certain ruts of negativity as allot of times we, no matter what, just don't want to admit that they're there. Most of the times it's because we're afraid of what we'll offset. We'll be either hurting ours or someone else's feelings in one way or another. We must except our feelings, however, we must also realize justice is justice no matter who is in the position of power. We are the power that will set us free, a good prayer doesn't hurt also.

Our positive attitude is basically our freedom from evil, this being a bad attitude. This doesn't of course mean that we deny facts though. We must recognize where our energies lie and feel where our power positions are. This will keep us moving ahead with a strategy for a positive attitude.

It's great that we can develop allot of knowledge about this or that, however with the wrong attitude we lose so much enjoyment and effectiveness. As we discussed earlier it's sometimes the result of a fear that is stopping us. Our goal then needs to be how to find a balance that is safe so we will beleive in ourselves and others. This will in turn allow others to beleive in us.

So how do we find that balance where it seems to just set us free. Well, first we have to specifically define what it is that we'll be offsetting as we go about our goals. We must also realize what present suffering we're experiencing as we move ahead towards our goals. If we realize our present suffering it should move us towards freedom which is what we deserve.

We deserve freedom and if we want to free ourselves of suffering we must develop a positive attitude so how do we develop a positive attitude? It's definitely not an easy task, if it was everyone would be happy and handle every situation perfectly. To develop a positive attitude we must think only positive thoughts.

There are only two ways of thinking, positively and negatively. We know we want freedom so we must think positively. Also, by freedom I'm indicating our dreams as dreams always give a sense of freedom. So think about a hot item and a cold item. How do they both make you feel? Well if we're thinking positively they should both make us feel positive. You could think of a nice relaxing hot tub, or a refreshing shower on a hot day, or even standing under a water fall in Fiji on a hot day.

No matter what is going on around us we must be able to turn it into a positive. Not to say we should place ourselves in dangerous situations which are immoral, unethical or dishonest and claim things are positive. We need to be realistic with our positive attitude, along with our morals, ethics, and honesty.

It's tough finding a balance with a positive attitude as we can be polite and positive, and people can misinterpret us, however if we remain positive we will explain the true meaning of how we're feeling. For example you may like a color and when you say you like a color someone might assume that you like that color on everything and everyone. Then the next thing you know they've told the whole world the wrong truth about our positive comment.

With our positive attitude we must figure out ways to relate it precisely to our listener. We can do this by recognizing three different ways of interpreting people. We have our viewpoint, someone else's, and the onlookers. To be balanced we must consider our situation and determine how we can relate to our listener using these three different viewpoints. Try it in your next conversation and notice how being aware makes for a more positive experience.

Now that we're considering different situations and viewpoints let's start to consider some ways to keep a positive attitude. Our physiology and how we feel and act. Even if we're not in the greatest of moods at the time, if we make an enormous physiological change along with a breathing change we'll instantly notice a change in our attitude. This of course should be towards the positive, right? You're awesome.

So let's look at a good example of a physiological change. Say we're driving and someone is about to turn into us as we're in there blind spot. We could either tense up and get negative, or maybe even panick. If we did the wrong thing we could create great havoc maybe even a large car pile up depending on where we are. However, if we start breathing properly, with a positive posture (physiology), and we focus on a safe spot to go, our internal senses will kick in and we'll head quickly to safety.

Now in this situation we're not going to become a hero or anything, however, we just made some serious shifts to take us to safety and fast. Our attitude is like that positive where we're heading towards our focus, negative where we're heading for destruction. It's similar to a hologram when we think positively or negatively. If we look at a hologram the wrong way we won't get the correct picture or thought. If we don't look at life with a positive attitude, we look at life in a negative way which quickly becomes a negative reality. When I say looking at life in a positive way I also mean looking at the principles of life in a positive way also. Things like morals, honesty, and ethics.

So as we're seeing with little invisible shifts we can really change the direction of our future. Time still is a factor, however the faster we change our attitude the faster we'll be heading in the correct direction. I mean who really wants to do anything that is going to take allot of work and effort. This is simply why allot of people don't set many challenging goals for themselves. To them setting a realistic goal with a positive attitude is almost worse than getting a tooth pulled.

This is really an odd situation though as when there's no reality people love to have goals. The reason is it seems so simple, and it just doesn't really matter, therefore many fears don't develop. Keeping a positive attitude is tough however we waste so much time with a negative attitude. With a positive attitude we're able to keep trying different ways to reach our goals. Then once we reach them we see how it was all worth it.

What we need to work on is maintain our positive attitude even when the going gets tough. By maintaining a positive attitude when the going gets tough keeps us mobile towards our goals. We must realize what we offset when we think positively on certain subjects. When more difficult situations arise that require us to keep a positive attitude we must first decide what's essential and what isn't. Then we must think about what we will offset with our positive attitude. For example if we already have a busy schedule and we want to invest more time in our computer campaign we must decide how thinking positively towards investing more time in our computer campaign will effect other areas. These other areas could be your social life, family life, or spiritual life.

Offsetting balance can change our whole personality for the positive or for the negative. We must of course make wise decisions that will only effect us for the positive. Yes of course we will all experience defeat at one time or another. We must with tact learn these seasons of disappointment.

So when it does come down to making critical decisions in critical times how can we handle it effectively? Well this is where we turn our whole life around. We basically use each situation as fuel for our fire. When it comes time to make a decision about our computer campaign or something else that is important we must be prepared to commit to being positive.

By committing to being positive we will enthusiastically get our other tasks done more meaningfully and effectively. This is the awesome part. The reason for this is efficiency. We've most likely done a task over and over many times, however due to attitude we let it take longer than it should. By changing our attitude to positive as a matter of importance we give a whole new meaning and dignity to our goal.

Now when we're working towards our successful computer campaign or whatever goal we may have we'll have the feeling of conquest as we're growing successfully towards our goals. This won't just be an empty talkers term, we'll be doing this in an honest, moral, and ethical way which will build us steam for success. This also develops competence for all areas of our life. The minute we become discouraged we lose all of our power, as it says in the bible. These are such true words so basically it's telling us that the minute we think negatively we lose our effectiveness.

Imagine you're in a race and you're in the number one position. You're running and running and starting to get abit tired. Then you're focused ahead on winning, however you look a little to the side and see a competitor. Now here you have two choices you can think positively or negatively. Either gain or lose power. You know the effect of thinking positively so you start to change things in you mind maybe you start to imagine that your his or her coach and trying to motivate your competitor to be as good as you.

Then next you change your physiology to one of empowerment you brain picks up the signal and then all of a sudden it's like you receive a massive burst of energy. You know how far to the finish line, so you pace yourself with your energy and start running faster. You competitor however didn't know the effectiveness of a positive attitude. The moment you changed your physiology and received that extra boost of energy your competitor picked up on it. He or she started to believe that they needed to in a position behind you to learn. They might not have done this consciously however they did it unconsciously. They then lost the thought or that there was one of passing you. You sure convinced them of this as you won the race. Congratulations, you're awesome.

I used this example here to indicate to you the power of attitude and its effectiveness. As you see it's in the most critical of moments where a superior psychology makes all the difference. This is where one becomes a success or a failure. You my friend are a success, you must grab hold of it within you and use it and watch it escape like a captive to freedom.

Think of all the most wonderful moments you've experienced in life and say "YES" to yourself in a positive and certain way. Now, do you want to experience all that life has to offer you, all the joys of life? Say "YES" and with a loud and positive tone. I believe in you and so do you. Life awaits your successes, now make it happen.

We've seen here how important it is to have a positive attitude. So many studies indicate that attitude makes such a difference, more than factual knowledge in many cases. This was shown where people with equal knowledge were tested. In these tests the ones who were believed in (and who weren't necessarily the smartest) developed the positive attitude and skills necessary to succeed. So you to can create a successful computer campaign for yourself using the success that lies within you. Make it happen.

Although most successes take time who knows what lies within you. Many successes have started with one simple move though, and that was because they had the attitude and believed in themselves. If we will only believe we can succeed with our computer campaign we will succeed, this might not happen as fast as we choose, however it will happen if you make it happen. So keep a balanced life and again make it happen for yourself.

About the Author

Esmonde is a diligent student of success. He has studied many forms of successes and failures over the last decade. The reason for this is allot of wisdom and knowledge may be obtained through both successes and failures in the development of achievement. Also, he believes if you're always studying success then you are only bound to be successful if you apply what you learn. This is similar to the saying you are what you eat, if you eat healthy you become healthy and vice versa. He knows that once anyone chooses a definite course that is passionate for them they are bound to attain it if they use an approach that's simple and practical for them.

Esmonde also with utmost respect and compassion believes in all of humankind for the better. He knows with certainty that anyone can drastically increase the quality of their life with simple shifts in behavior. He also knows that many people coast along in life with no direction, whether it be because their in the "loop of success" (i.e.: they just can't improve themselves anymore) or because they just haven't made a clear enough decision. Allot of times decisions are made due to lack of ones believe in themselves and their abilities. With his definite attitude (though it's not guaranteed as your success depends on you) you are bound to see many positive changes in your day to day life if you apply the few simple principles he teaches. This is also in addition to his unstoppable certain and committed belief in you the reader.